Loving Your Shadow

Julia Brandenstein

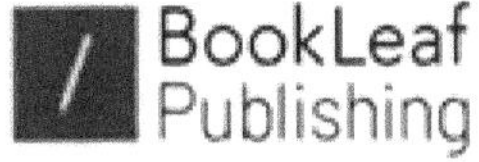

Presentation by *BookLeaf Publishing*

Web: www.bookleafpub.com

E-mail: info@bookleafpub.com

ISBN: 9789357213363

First edition 2023

Your Own War

The battle against oneself
has always been the hardest
because begging yourself to stay
and saying no
is a rejection
hard to place in words.
It feels as if there is no set of eyes
kind enough
to want to beg you to stay.
The ripping of the seams of your soul
was always so hard to bare
when it was so loud to you
and so soft to others.
Your heart and mind feel so fleeting
almost as if
even they too, do not want to stick around
for you.
Even when you hold hands
with the desire to stay
you must remember,
your arms are weak when not supported.

Smoke

Sometimes it would hurt to smoke.
It hurt to smoke
when the pull hit my throat
and I felt every cell simply choke
but it wasn't until you said to me
that you needed to leave
that I knew what it was like
to choke
or to have the air
ripped from your lungs
just like the exhales
that used to burn before the air
of your words
entered my lungs

Pain

pain is a word
used to describe the feeling
of the cold wind on your skin
for those who could go home
the pit of hunger
for those who could eat again
the feelings of loneliness
for those who would see loved ones again
but could never define
the way that my own mind
made me feel
as the absence of my spirit
left me hollow,
for a different pain to fill

Dusk

Here we sit together
in the era of my dusk
where the world is no longer as bright,
but there is enough light
just to keep moving.
Its like drowning
right above the surface
so everyone can hear you
everyone can see you
but there is no reason to run
because to them
you are at the surface.

I miss you

I miss you
they say
in every call and text
in every soft spoken voice
trying to see what happened
to the version of you
they say they miss.
But there is no hate
more bitter than for the people
who think they miss you
more than you miss yourself.
I miss her too.
I wish for her too.
I pray for her too.

Longer

There were many times
I asked how much longer
in between each fight with death
you wonder when will it take me
maybe someday
maybe the next day
but the rule of rivers
is that they never run dry,
More blood must always be spilt

the cause

if I keep writing
about our love
if I keep saying
it was real
it continues on
in my memory
like the phases
of the moon
and even when you
can't see it
I know
it will always
be there

unfinished

8

I can no longer
bare
to look into
your eyes
and see the remains
of a love poem,
unfinished,
but no longer mine

winter

her womb
was cold
for her healing had stopped
and the woman
she was
ran barren
and dry,
for that string of hope
was no longer enough
for her to hold onto

happiness

now that I have seen happiness
written on a face
like yours
there is nothing else I grieve
more than your smile
when expressing how
you
are my happiness

for me

for me
is what they always said
stay for me
please
they prayed with sad eyes.
With a narrow smile
they asked what
could have been so bad.
For you I want to scream back
for you I dare to yell in their face
for you I ache to pound on the table
for you?
the slits on my wrist
don't burn for you
by grief in my heart
doesn't hurt for you
the tears in my eyes
don't fall for you
because nothing
was ever
for you it was her
the girl who cried and cried
as the world nearly watched her die
and she considered going to the other side
every day but all you do

is sit and ask for me?
no.
for her

for her

I stayed for the feeling of
holding my degree,
of the congratulation of a first job,
to hear me ring the keys of a new apartment
to hold a new dog,
to feel the sun on my back,
to hold my childs hand,
to walk down my aisle,
to feel my happiness,
to feel the light inside,
to bring myself joy,
to make myself laugh,
to feel myself love again.
not for you. not for anyone.
for her

hollow

the ghost of the girl
I used to be
followed this body around
until she was ready
to join with it again
and spend the rest of
this life
with herself

short

for all the dreams
I dreamed of living
I told my soul
to carry on
even without me there
to keep those alive.
Life is too short
to let my fleeting dreams
die

spring to her

the spring always
brought me back to her
as the suns rays
pierced through thick
winter ice
melting away
letting the world blossom
reminding her
no season
was forever

.

We know what happened
This is a safe place for you
Tell us just once more
nothing will happen
but it happens so fast.

I just spilled my guts
Every heart wrenching detail
Was now all of theirs
as pen to paper
documented how your life changed
before your eyes.

I wanted to cry as I saw
Their paperwork just said she
Like I had no name
and wasn't even real

And I know
poems like these
are hard to read
but you have no idea
how hard it is to live
when you are 'she
Poem 17: fear

Please don't leave me
And make me fight against this cruel world on
my own
With "I didn't want to hurt you" as your last
words
Because if you do
I'll hurt

And I'll recite this poem
until it is carved into your heart
And we both forget how to breathe
And you'll say
"I'm sorry. Love you."

And I'll say
"Ok"

whisper please

don't stare at me
With that smile of yours
Because when you do
My heart can't help but flutter
Please don't sit under the starry sky
Because when your eyes touch the light
I'll think we can have forever

Please don't hug me when I'm down
And let me sink into your warm embrace
Because when you rub soothing circles into my
hand
I'll actually believe you won't let go

Please don't talk above a whisper when you are
here
Because my parents will always hear
And they will tell me how amazing you are
And what a shame it would be to lose you

meeting

his soul held mine
like a mother
to a child
his laugh tender
to my ears
which had never heard
kind words
and I knew
his touch
was the one
to mend my scars

him

he was the warm glimmer
of a candle against the wall
and the gentle breeze of august
that made the world feel
like part of it
was meant for you

for k

I imagine
in some other universe
your eyes are what every star
looks like
and your soul is the inspiration
for every beautiful thing
and your laugh
is what moves through the flowers
and that your memory is somewhere
I can visit forever

www.ingramcontent.com/pod-product-compliance
Lightning Source LLC
LaVergne TN
LVHW050306200726
843509LV00015B/3197